One Love,
Jessica Burns
2022

INTRODUCTION

The process of this book began several years ago when I recognized there were emotions from my childhood showing up in my adult life that needed peeling away, forgiveness, and healing. Gratefully, I now understand that **all** experiences life provides are necessary for our self-awareness and evolution. *Golden Guidance* is a compilation of reflections and affirmations created from the process of working through my emotional cloudiness to find clarity and inner peace. My intention for anyone reading this book is to help inspire growth through life's challenges and to affirm faith, belief in oneself, and the alignment with God is always available. I encourage everyone to connect with the signals that guide and use the unlimited power of personal energy, thoughts, and words to impact inner change.

I dedicate this book to my Mom [Gail], who most recently acknowledged that she is grateful I survived my childhood, and my Husband [Mr. Burns] and Son's [Kenny III & Kyle] as they were the catalyst for the beginning of my shift within.

Forever growing, Jessica Burns

B REATHE *life* into anything you want to create; MANIFESTATIONS NEED YOUR *MAGIC*.

Show up *authentic* in relationships to **establish the foundation** for something *authentic* to keep.

OWN YOUR ENERGY.

LET GO ***of the people, thoughts, situations and feelings*** that do not serve your wellness, happiness or wholeness.

E stablish *boundaries* with yourself and others. They are necessary for a healthy life and will support **emotional balance** for your mind, body and spirit.

Think less, *feel* more;
allow your QUIET
INTUITION to guide you
and your process.

TAME your ego and be open to a *perspective other than your own*.

The information you *receive* may **provide the answers** you seek.

C ovet your *happiness.*

The *beauty* of KARMA responds to ***every action***, regardless if we believe the act, energy or words to be right or wrong.

G rateful for days
filled with loving
moments, easy
conversations, endless
laughter, **memories made
for a lifetime** and especially
the *people* in our lives that
make it all real.

B E *inspired* by the success of others and also *guided* by their challenges. Recognizing that the [*work in between*] is our responsibility and will require our own *unique effort, dedication and focus.*

Embrace the **tough days**, they exist for necessary *reflection*, growth and GUIDANCE.

WHEN you feel incapable, ***choose*** to push through and forward. CHOOSE to *override* the negative thoughts that can become our own mental cage.

D iscern and define
the *status* and
boundaries of your
relationships.

Not everyone
deserves or has earned
unlimited *access to you or
your energy*.

FOCUSING on what you
don't have, who doesn't
like or support you and the
negative aspects of your
past and present are a **waste
of mental energy**. You
cannot manifest a positive
life with a negative mindset.
Choose yourself, honor your
experiences, accept where
you are and move forward
with gratitude for change.

Courage and honesty will always SUPPORT you to *say* what needs to be *said* and ***do*** what needs to be ***done***.

Compassion will allow you to walk in another person's shoes, while ***lifting*** their embarrassment, pain, suffering or discomfort.

Learn to see outside of yourself; **at some point,** *we all struggle to be who we are.*

N ever
underestimate
the person who
fears only GOD.

ALWAYS lead with *love* and *kindness*, while also maintaining boundaries to not allow others to manipulate, mistreat or marginalize you.

Success in life is not based on one significant moment; just as one **failure** does not represent a failed life and determine our destiny. The ability to celebrate each level of our wins and also pivot from disappointments, is the necessary balance to *harmoniously* manage life's highs and lows.

The *perfect* upbringing
was not yours to begin
with. The tainting of your
self-worth started ***before
your awareness of it***. You
are not the faults of your
family or those from your
formative years. You were
born to break the cycle, to
change the story and the
direction of your life.

WE are consistently reminded of where we stand in our relationships through **actions and energy**. ALLOW actions and energy, instead of explanations and empty conversations to *reveal clarity*. We cannot change the choices made by others, only be informed by them.

ALTHOUGH the programming from childhood made you feel unseen and unheard, **choose to take up space and make your presence known.** We are all children of GOD and are HERE to be seen, felt and heard.

A S much as we want the people in our lives to be a part of our journey, **recognize not everyone is ready to mutually participate**. Wish them well and pray that their *own alignment will support their growth* and meet you back on your life path.

FORGIVENESS guides us toward **emotional freedom** and protects our *inner glow*. More energy is drained to maintain a space of heaviness than it does to rise above and float in ***happiness***.

GRATEFUL *for **all***
relationships; good, bad,
loving and toxic. Every
experience has the potential
to evolve our life toward our
highest self and purpose.

Our strength, truth and
character would not be
discovered without
the push and pull of the
ever-changing people in our lives.

You are never alone. There is and will always be a *higher power* present to support you and your version of success.

Set your *focus* in
the **direction** of your
dreams.

The only thing you lack is forgetting to remind yourself daily that **you lack nothing** at all. ABUNDANT MIND and *life.*

The same people that want to **dim** *your light* are often the same people that want to **use your light** for their own gain, use and control.

GROWTH;
the uncomfortable,
emotional and at times
painful **process** of
identifying the root cause
of behavior patterns that
negatively impact ourselves
and others. This discovery
and awareness, provides
the foundation for the
alchemical power to create
change within and evolve.

A fractured spirit is no excuse to live resentful and bitter; take your *power back* as GOD keeps all the records.

SOUL [chosen] *family*; not related by blood, but connected by the alignment of love, respect, joy, encouragement, trust and understanding.

RELATIONSHIPS that collapse are meant to fall away. Those that stay connected are supposed to remain. GOD's ***divine plan is consistent***, as every door closed leads to another door to be opened. Our relationships are given for a REASON, SEASON OR LIFETIME.

IN life, relationship betrayals and failures will occur; however, the most detrimental betrayal and failure is of **SELF**.

LOVING OURSELVES MORE than the pains caused by disappointing relationships *activates the* POWER that allows us to heal, overcome, forgive and flow ***forward***.

FAITH is *revealed*
through how we
choose to spiritually
and physically show
up for ourselves;
align within to be
guided and supported
through those times
when faith is needed
and tested the most.

If everything went our way, we would not be **challenged** and **pushed** to EVOLVE into who *we are meant to be*.

MENTALLY [MIND], *physically* [BODY] and **spiritually** [SPIRIT] play and enjoy the game of *LIFE*.

Our *full body of work* defines who we are. UNAPOLOGETICALLY OWN life's ebbs and flows; the opinions and judgments of others do not determine or create our reality.

There will be moments in life that *forever change who you are*. Pray and trust that the change is leading you to your highest self.

TO *become* a better version of yourself, you need to SEE and BELIEVE that a **higher version of you exists**; change doesn't occur while holding onto the energy of your current or past mistakes.

The *perfect life* is also a life with **challenges** and consistent *change*.

The tight grip on your goals will not make them actualize any faster; **ground your emotions**, trust the process, and *allow faith* to flow and guide your manifestations.

Although there are moments when we feel our **insecurities**, choose to believe *you are always enough.*

R elationships evolve and develop in various ways. Although the energy exchanges are not the same, it doesn't remove the **prayers**, **love** and **peace** you wish for those once a part of your journey.

The idea of **perfection is limited** to a specific outcome and a specific moment in time. *LIFE* is FOREVER learning, growing and creating until we are no longer on this earth; *our perfect legacy is a life fully lived.*

ONE-SIDED relationships will no longer serve a purpose when you **_understand your self-worth_** and the _value_ of your time, energy and effort.

Practice *happiness.*

LOVE and *HONOR your truth* not only the good but also the shadows. ACCEPTANCE **and** AWARENESS OF SELF is essential to guide and support your evolution and understanding that you are complete and whole.

Believe
in *the good of people*
until they show
themselves different.

Accessing **LOVE** and **GRACE**, guides us to recognize *what to say and do* in all moments of life.

Y OUR MAGIC
of gifts, talents
and creativity *are*
never diminished or
depleted when you
teach what you know.

Be patient with your growth. Not everyone comes into this world on the same level playing field; some were given more life tools, love and support than others.

Be proud at every new revelation and **honor every time you chose to elevate**; your life journey is supporting the vision you see for yourself.

To *find* the truth,
follow the actions.

It's not about adapting with the times, it's about being dedicated and *consistent* with your OWN *growth* and *process*.

We didn't *grow, ascend* and *progress* this far to remain stagnant and not experience *LIFE in full bloom*.

KEEP GOING.

Being a BLESSING *to others* will always and forever be the ***real blessing.***

S tay true to *who you are*. Those who recognize your **gifts** will see, honor and appreciate them.

It is the **essence of who you are** that distinguishes each of us as individuals. *The energy you radiate is unique*; while others may copy and paste, it will never resonate or be the same because *you are your magic.*

W e all have **something**
special within that is
irreplaceable.

Stay in the *flow of alignment*. When the energy of people and moments feel off, notice the signal to pause and be *open* to pivot in another direction.

NOT interested in competing with anyone; we all **benefit** when *we all make it.*

S ometimes we give it our all and the outcome is not what we expected. Remember, *every experience contains a valuable lesson, leads us forward and is never a wasted moment.*

Focus and
INTENTION
allows your path to
unfold and provide
everything you *need*.

WE are meant to *go through* everything we've gone through; our **SOUL** is navigating the direction of where we need to be.

LOSE the *emotion* -
keep the passion.

The **DREAM** is *real*.

We can find
something
wrong when we
are *constantly
looking for it.*

Your *life* is your
lane, ***pace***
and ***race***.

We are never lost, ***living life*** is the journey of **finding ourselves**.

THERE is never a need to take the actions of others personal. THE level of energy others emanate is the *energy* they possess within.

The simplest
moments are
the *true joys* of
life.

LIFE experiences and relationships **run their course** because our SPIRIT is needing something *more*.

LISTEN, **feel** and *integrate* the knowledge from the lesson.

Our ALIGNMENT is
necessary to receive
inner guidance,
spiritual grounding
and creative
inspiration for a
boundless life.

Giving our energy and
attention to what everyone
else is thinking or doing
disconnects our alignment.

G OOD with
yourself
allows you to
be good with
everyone else.

ACHIEVING success and reaching GOALS can feel uncomfortable and unworthy while overcoming life challenges; *celebrate and embrace every win,* as what we have worked for and earned is abundantly deserved.

When our *spirit* is
right, there is never a
need to chase the
                light.

The energy of complaining will prevent progress and elevation. ACCESS ***gratitude as the gateway*** to move through the challenges and toward the solutions for change.

Don't **_lose yourself_** in trying to fulfill and meet the expectations of *others.*

EVERYTHING is
possible.

In this LIFE *we get what we give*. Never allow your expectations to exceed your efforts.

CHOOSE the
energy of *love* over
the energies of
fear, greed, anger
or jealousy. Our
thoughts and **feelings**
become our ***words***
and ***actions;*** we don't
always RECOVER from
what was said or
done.

Some of our toughest
challenges are learned
behavior [generational
curses]. In reflection,
the origin of these
patterns can be
identified to those
that are **connected
with our lives**; feel it,
heal it, release it and
evolve from it.

You are solely
responsible for your
happiness, **peace** and
emotional wellness.
Everything will fall
into place when you
take care of you.

Obsessing, judging
or questioning how
others live their lives
is a **valueless use
of time and energy**.
Our choices refuel
or drain us, choose
wisely.

*O*wn *your* **superpowers.**

*A*lways be
READY.

RESPECT
over
fame.

S tay **true** to your
gifts and **follow**
your inner guidance.

Save **YOURSELF**
and
wish them well.

The ego is
never satisfied.

The greatest *love* is from within. *Self-love* provides the inner **resilience** to ACTUALIZE the dreams in our hearts.

Confusion often shows up from a lack of self awareness, and not trusting and knowing who we are. *Honoring and appreciating our true self and process will provide the gift of clarity.*

SHARING our journey, lessons and discovered gifts, allows us to recognize the *beauty in the struggle;* **we are all connected through our common experiences.**

You are *worth* it.

Everything needed to
fulfill our dreams is
already within. Our
VALUE is innate.
BELIEVE and know
that you have *enough
within* to accomplish
it all.

BE *authentic*.

BE **consistent**.

BE *honest*.

L<small>EAN IN</small> to challenges and grow through the lessons; *life* is THE *best teacher.*

There are times when **all that can be done has been done**, and what remains is the CHOICE to let go or be caged by what no longer serves the spirit.

THE **TRUTH** will always *find us.*

It is not our responsibility to change the people in our lives. *We are* SOLELY *responsible for ourselves* and **how we choose to engage**.

We don't have
haters,
the **LOVE** *is*
misdirected.

Be mindful of the expectations we place on each other, as we can only show up **at the level of our existence**.

The *emotional capacity* to extend beyond who we are, or who we need others to be, may not be developed within. MEET **people where they are**.

Regardless of
your *success*
always maintain
a GENEROUS and
GRATEFUL ***heart.***

A LLOW *peace*
and *wisdom*
to replace
the empty spaces
remaining from
our struggles and
survival.

What we need for our *spirit* and want for our **ego** are not the same. *Trust* the inner guidance to always ***reveal the difference***.

B ELIEVE *to*
   receive.

WISDOM *is gained* when we find the courage to let go of what no longer serves us and get out of our own [ego] way. Every lesson we're not open to learn from, will show up again to be repeated and revealed in another form.

There is always another *level*. EVOLVE *or* **repeat**.

GRATITUDE

WILL SAVE YOU from complaining, doubting and blaming.

FORGIVENESS does not equal full access. Allowing the *same level of interaction* to satisfy your ego, only gives permission to **repeat the same mistake and betrayal**.

WHEN we remain **stuck in the emotion,** we miss the opportunities to LOVE, HONOR and EMBRACE our *survival*, *growth* and *power*.

Your ENERGY never lies
or will be denied because
you have chosen to walk
in your AUTHENTIC truth
and PURPOSE. Your gifts
and MAGIC they carry will
continue to leave a legacy
imprint of *love*, *integrity*,
strength and *leadership*.

B E more concerned about **karma** and *manifesting a great life* than giving attention and reacting to the energy of judgment, betrayals and disappointments.

Trust that everything
will be okay, the
vision you see for
yourself is *greater*
than your darkest days.

Our ENERGY *is life giving* – **focus on creating solutions** to the challenges and not the challenges alone.

D on't allow the **thoughts in your head** to keep you from manifesting the inspiration you *feel in your heart.*

YOUR sense of **worthiness** is not contingent upon how others *chose to interact with or treat you.*

Friendships *endure* when we remain open with *compassion* and ACCEPT *the realness* of our individual truths.

The **life** of your
dreams, lives
within the *change*
you resist.

IN SPITE of a past
that has taught
you to expect less,
**always remember
you deserve** *peace of
mind, happiness* and
unconditional love.

KEEP it *real* with YOURSELF so there is never a need to fake it with others.

Allowing yourself to
be happy is just as
important as *choosing
to feel happiness*.

Peace of mind and FREEDOM exists in the **choice** we have over our *perspectives* and *attitudes*.

Truly a **blessing** when you reflect and realize that not everyone will make the journey and be where GOD *is taking you*.

ALIGN *yourself with the future and its dreams.* **Let go of the past and its disappointments.**

IN spite of a world that values what you do or have [material] over character [spiritual]; understand that **CHARACTER** will serve as solid ground when the *fluctuations of material life **change*** how others love, see and treat you.

Our past mistakes aren't meant to reduce personal value. Challenges arrive in our life to teach, provide clarity and reveal more *of who we truly are.*

Trust your journey
and embrace life's
pleasures and pains
as *equal* **EVOLUTION**
opportunities.

GROWTH
activates our
strength and
power.

MEET **people where they are** with *zero expectations,* and always LEAD WITH LOVE.

LOVE and SUPPORT *without judgment*, we are all striving **toward our own version of greatness**.

ALIGN *within and release the need for others to be in agreement with your vision and goals.*

MORE **connections** *with* and **guidance** *from*
GOD.

R esist allowing your past to anchor your soul. Choose to remain PRESENT and **free.**

Although others may not want to acknowledge your evolution and **see only the past version of you**, no one can take away the WORK you've done *toward your growth*.

GROWTH doesn't make us better or less than others; our **individual journeys are** *divinely unique*.

PRAY that the
conflicts people take
you through aren't in
vain. Remain hopeful
that the **lessons are
a necessary step in
their journey** and will
support their *growth*
for future healthy
relationships.

At PEACE with *everything,* so now I'm **going after everything**.

The ATTRIBUTES we see and feel when connecting with others also lives within ourselves. Due to past conditioning and emotional traumas, our own qualities are often buried so deep that we don't recognize the beauty that lives within. **KEEP HEALING.**

Never allow the negative chatter from others to distract you from your goals. People often criticize *what they don't understand*, *what they have yet to accomplish*, while also **questioning how you got it done**.

Actions and words rooted in guilt are not in alignment with our true self. **Guilt is a low vibrational energy**, and although the intention is good, the outcome will be empty.

The *prayers and hopes* for our family, friends and loved ones will always have more **spiritual impact** than the energy of our worries, judgments and complaints.

I will have TRUSTING relationships because *I trust myself*.

I will have LOYAL relationships because *I am loyal to myself*.

I will FORGIVE others because *I have forgiven myself*.

I will SPEAK TRUTH to others because *I speak truth to myself*.

I will be a BLESSING to others because *I have blessed myself*.

I will UNCONDITIONALLY LOVE others because *I unconditionally love myself.*

HEALING activates with
our choices. The therapy,
affirmations and lessons
are only the **beginning of
the process.** The real work
begins when life tests us the
most and we INTEGRATE and
IMPLEMENT the *spiritual tools
with compassion, love and
grace.*

Set your
HEART
in the *right direction*

ALTHOUGH you have been disappointed and failed by others, you can choose not to *fail yourself.* LET GO of replaying the negative thoughts and emotions of what was or could have been. GIVE **yourself permission to be free**.

DURING the times
of darkness,
remember to find
the *GLIMMERS OF
LIGHT.*

Our LIFE may not always go the way it was planned; however, there is never a need to allow the moments of insecurity, disappointment and fear keep you from *seeing* your own **greatness**.

REFLECT and
become your own
SOURCE of
LIGHT.

Leave the judgment
of others up to GOD.
Focus on VISUALIZING
your higher self and
dreams.

ALLOW yourself to
meet life where your
VISION is *leading you*.

BE mindful of
how you move in
this world. WE can't
reverse the moment
of **what was said** or
*how we made
someone feel*.

Gratitude, **_compassion,_** forgiveness, **grace** and _patience_ are all acts of love.

OWN the responsibilities of your choices, creative endeavors and happiness; *blessed with the beauty of free will* – we only **limit ourselves.**

GRATITUDE is the *gateway*.

IN every *minute, hour, day, week, month* and *year* there is an **opportunity to start again.**

LOVE will *always* be the **answer**.

WE ALL want and deserve *unconditional love* and appreciation.

LOVE yourself enough to **discern between** receiving love only when conditions are met and *LOVE UNCONDITIONAL*.

MORE time *loving* and *living life*. LESS time observing and judging the lives of others.

Our work and
life appears
effortless when
we pour our love
and energy into
everything we do.

DISCERN between
faux pleasantries
and
AUTHENTIC
CONNECTIONS.

SELECTIVE – not only
with the **material aspects
of life** such as the food we
eat, the clothes we wear
and the people we choose
to spend time with, but
also with the *spiritual
aspects of life*, our
thoughts, the words we
speak and the energy we
keep around and within.

The *realest friendships* offer LOVE and EMPATHY through the challenges, and not give the dark moments the permanent power to love each other any less.

LIFE decisions are best *guided intuitively*; NO book, research study, family member or friend can concisely **determine what provides you joy, fulfillment and happiness.**

What doesn't serve our *energy*, doesn't deserve our *energy*.

GRATITUDE allows
us to receive the gift
of disappointment;
how we ***chose to
move forward*** has the
POWER to either trap
or evolve us.

To see the *LIGHT* in others is to **acknowledge** the *LIGHT we see in ourselves.*

What feeds our **ego** *will not feed or sustain our* SPIRIT.

B LESSED STATE OF MIND.

Claim your birthright of *happiness*, **love** and **accept** yourself as GOD's divine creation.

We all have the **power to evolve** when we *embrace*, *own* and *love* our truth.

WE can MANIFEST it **all**
when ***divine timing*** is *allowed
to order our steps.*

We spend so much time trying to *live up to the expectations of others* that we begin to **unconsciously shrink the authentic parts of ourselves** – leading to a cycle of self judgment and limited belief in who we are.

DEPROGRAM the past to *fully live and create* a new narrative in the PRESENT NOW.

THOSE that remind us to honor ourselves and celebrate us, **even when we choose not to**, are *life's walking angels*.

B ECAUSE *you are irreplaceable*, always teach what you have learned.

N ever a need to *dim,* HIDE or *neglect* your **LIGHT**.

GIVE to others the grace, love and compassion they need in order to *receive from others* the grace, love and compassion we need.

FOCUS on the goal with faith–filled flexibility; know it is always okay and often necessary to *step back*, **realign** and PIVOT.

WE often judge and compare others for *who they are* and **who they are not** from a limited and uninformed perspective – without *empathy* or *knowledge* of another's journey from child to adult.

AN acknowledgment of another's greatness is not a dismissal of your own light. CHECK–IN with your feelings; the ***personal wins are unlimited*** and there is never a need to hold space for envy or insecurity.

RELATIONSHIP status should be clarified and defined. The LEVEL at which *energy is exchanged and reciprocated* provides the advice to understand the relationship's nature and informs us to know how much energy to give.

Focusing on what you
don't have, who doesn't
accept you and your past
mistakes is a misuse of
the energy needed
         *to create unlimited
                possibilities.*

D iscernment will support you in recognizing what *matters the most* and what is **irrelevant**.

SELF *acceptance*
and *love* will forever
begin ***within***.

CONSISTENCY is a
mindful practice to
support and **sustain**
the relationship with
ourself and others.

B e *patient with your growth*.
The struggles and
behavior patterns that
challenge us most,
were **unconsciously
learned** from as early
as our childhood.

When feeling unsure, use this as a sign to be **still** and **align** *with* GOD; the *answers you need will arrive at the perfect time.*

You *claim your*
FREEDOM when you
speak your truth.

TO EXIST and remain in a state of unhappiness **reflects a lack of self-love and forgiveness of the past.** Find the courage and strength to heal the pain; you are deserving of all that is good.

Remember to
feed your spirit
everyday.

U se the broken
pieces of the past
as **building blocks**
for *the spiritual
foundation* to support
your healing, growth
and assist with
reaching your fullest
potential.

GOD, SOURCE,
the CREATOR, *the*
UNIVERSE or the
HIGHER POWER, *will*
bring to light any and
everything that **needs**
to be revealed.

Self-*LOVE* is
the embodiment
of *forgiveness*,
grace, **discipline**,
boundaries and
authenticity.

NEVER allow others to minimize your progress, self-worth, success and goals because you did not *FOLLOW* **their ideal expectations, opinions, plans and standards.**

Make PEACE with the disappointments of your past relationships, *if they are destined to return*, those relationships will meet you **back on your journey**.

LOVE and SUPPORT without judgment; we are all on the journey to **rise** from the falls and to *love* after the heartbreaks.

The most important ALIGNMENT and CONNECTION is with GOD to our *mind, body and spirit*.

BE MINDFUL of pride and ***open to the viewpoint*** of others. The GUIDANCE provided may not be the message you wanted to hear; however, the *divine wisdom* you **needed to receive**.

I N THE MIDST of problem solving, *focus your energy* on the *solutions*.

What you do [material] should never be valued over *who you are* [spiritual].

The BELIEF others have in you and your potential is **limited** to how much *belief you have* and ***vision you see*** for yourself.

*Operate solely
from a place of
LOVE,
anything less
is self betrayal.*

YOU DESERVE
all that is great simply
because you *allowed*
yourself to receive it.

LOVE yourself and
the *rest will follow*.

LIFE can be as complex or as simple as you make it, and the seasons of change are forever consistent. IN THE MIDST OF IT ALL – remember to create days filled with gratitude, love and happiness.

When we **compare** ourselves to others, we **limit** our *unique potential* and **dim** our own light.

Choosing FORGIVENESS and *self-love* will always **return** your power back to you.

BEAUTIFUL
thing when you can *simultaneously* send someone LOVE and send them on their way.

Consider sending
prayers BEFORE
negative energy
when betrayed
and disrespected.
Remember when you
are ALIGNED and GOOD
with yourself, there's
*never a need to hurt
others.*

Congratulate yourself daily. Your next move will always bring you CLOSER to *where you need to be.*

Make **PEACE** with
your past and
    allow *PEACE to
lead your future*.

PAST mistakes aren't
meant to reduce
our personal value.
CHALLENGES arrive in life to
teach, PREPARE and **guide** us
toward our inner evolution.

CLARIFY your
INTENTIONS,
define your vision
and **set your goals**.

RELATIONSHIPS
that are valued and
based on **material
transactions** offer
very little for the
heart to receive.

S TAY *hydrated*, so there is never a need to be thirsty.

ACTIONS *reveal* the true INTENTIONS of any *unclear* relationship.

OUR *surroundings do not determine* our state of being. CHOOSE to *fill* the most negative spaces with your LOVE and LIGHT.

THE ego is strong and pride is a slippery slope of truth and perspective. DESPITE how many words are said to justify our missteps, cognitive dissonance won't erase the truth of the past. ACKNOWLEDGMENT of the wrong and CHANGED behavior are the resolutions to ***move forward.***

WE all fall short, not give our best and disappoint ourselves and others. Make **PEACE** with the experience, FORGIVE and move forward with the *lessons to create inner change.*

Remember to believe, accept, appreciate, honor and love **YOURSELF**, *as much as* you believe, accept, appreciate, honor and love ***others***.

OUR *journeys are unique and divine.* THE process of GROWTH and HEALING cannot be limited or judged.

SOME PHASES of life and parts of ourselves aren't always beautiful and yet still *deserving* of **love**, **honor** and **respect**. ALWAYS give *love*, *honor* and *respect* to the potential within.

NOT every relationship is meant to be; however, there is good inside each of us. **COMPASSION** has the gift to *reveal* the higher version of ourselves when negativity takes hold. Discovering the core of who we are and the cause of our past pains allows us to ***break free from negative patterns and elevate.***

When we worry, we bind and limit the energy that *allows our faith to work* on our behalf and for those we **LOVE.**

We are all *blessed with* LIFE so the works of GOD can be seen, felt and heard. We all have a *divine* **purpose**.

LEARN to depend on
yourself; **TRUST** your
INSTINCTS and *follow your
own path.*

When *ALIGNED*,
no one can ***lead
you*** as good as
you.

There is never a
need to match the
**energy or actions
received** from others
as KARMA naturally
settles the difference.

WE learn what needs to be **healed** within from what *emotionally triggers* us the most.

WISDOM *from our soul* *is always available.*

TO *LOVE is to also know pain.* There is a **process of grief** when relationships end or are forced to change because the bonds held together by love are broken.

*The mirror reveals a
beautiful truth of our
inner potential and
will provoke emotions
within, leading
us toward honest
reflection and growth.*

WHEN *life* gives us
what we don't want,
take the opportunity
to see **life calling** on
us to pause and ***move***
in another direction.

FORGIVE others and most importantly yourself. The TRUTH of our journey is wrapped in all of the lessons and blessings of a ***past we can never change.***

We are all meant to evolve, and for some, your growth may cause those to perceive and treat you different. No need to take the reactions personal as everyone's path is an individual process guided by the *choice* to accept change or remain the same.

Your *Life*,

your MAGIC.

PEACE of mind, body and spirit should not occur at the expense of pleasing others. PEACE is not the absence of conflict, but the *choice* to honor our worthiness over the lack of love and respect displayed by others.

CONFLICT may arise; however, **choose to engage only when disagreements are met with love and respect.**

*T*HERE are some
that will choose
to see you through
their own perspective.
ALWAYS *remain
grounded in who you
are and release the
need to control what
others say, think or
believe.*

FOLLOW your
own path;
create your *own*
blueprint.

PAST pains don't need
to live in our present.
Create the space within
and *believe* you are
enough – you deserve
to be ***loved***, ***seen*** and
heard.

WORDS CARRY ENERGY.
Choose the words you
use wisely. LIFE *is the
reflection* of what we
feel and speak.

The ***healing process*** will
present new life situations
that feel like deep wounds
from the past. Although
uncomfortable, the
emotions can be a useful
catalyst to understand,
forgive, love and *emotionally*
set ourselves free.

THE END of close relationships can feel like a hole in our spirit from the broken connection. ALLOW yourself to grieve, acknowledge the loss and *release* what once was, knowing that **life continues** and **love always remains** within.

The *QUALITY* of our
relationships can
be measured by the
levels of respect,
love, compassion and
honesty exchanged.

Pay attention to
   what resonates
with your spirit. This
guidance shows up to
confirm what we know,
**remind what we
forgot** or TEACH WHAT
WE NEED TO LEARN.

CHARACTER is revealed and shown through our *small daily actions.* THE thoughts, words and energy exchanges are **important details of life** – AS WE ARE WHAT WE REPEATEDLY DO.

WE are brought *through* the fire not for defeat but for **REBIRTH.** EVERY test brings us closer to our *higher self.*

O ur **wholeness** is felt within when we *fully* LOVE and APPRECIATE who we are AND also *celebrate* the wins of others as if there were our very own.

TO recognize and accept the root CAUSE of our emotional trauma, pain and behavior patterns, **while also having the strength and courage to heal**, is the *blessing of a lifetime*.

HOLDING on to who we were and our past failures won't *allow* the VISION of our UNLIMITED SELF to establish roots and *flourish*.

When trying to *reopen* **closed doors,** REMEMBER how that past experience made you feel.

Through words and actions we are **consistently reminded** where we stand and the status of our relationships. *CLOSURE to accept the reality*, is needed only within ourselves.

LOVE and *positive energy* can mend the connection of our broken relationships; understanding those responsible for the breaking are also ***responsible for the rebuilding***.

RELATIONSHIPS that **deplete our energy** bring attention to not only decrease interaction or let go of, but also to LOVE and CARE for *ourselves more.*

The power of **LOVE,**

the power of PEACE,

the power of *GRACE,*
and
the power of PRAYER,

are always accessible within.

Returning all
negative WORDS and
the ENERGY they
carry *back to sender*,
they are no longer
welcomed here.

To be aligned
and in flow is
the *energy* felt when
**connected with the
higher power**.

ALIGNMENT allows
us to feel our own
limitless possibilities
and potential.
Alignment is the goal.

Be *brave* enough to
SPEAK your truth,
rather than ***suffocate***
in silence.

Our bodies are energetically connected to our emotions. The ability to vibrationally express how we feel is a gift. BE responsible for the energy you bring; *what we give is always returned.*

Comparing ourselves to how others live their lives **dilutes and drains our creative power**. NURTURE yourself to expand the energy fundamental to *designing the life of your dreams.*

WHAT YOU CREATE *should be guided by and filled with your unique spirit and authentically reflect and represent you.*

GIVE *compassion* and care to others but not at the **detriment or sacrifice of yourself.**

Advice is good; however, our SOUL *always knows* what we *need*.

LIVE the EXAMPLE
*so the opinions of others
are irrelevant.*

ALTHOUGH we can give guidance and encourage others to evolve and heal. GOD through *life* **is the only true teacher**. We do not own the responsibility of when and how others choose to integrate support and elevate their lives.

HEAL

LOVE

FORGIVE

BALANCED relationships offer a *reciprocal exchange* of LIFE supporting energy, love and grace. THEY are life's *invaluable gifts* and *blessings.*

We are all intrinsically **whole** and embody love, truth and happiness.

Self-doubt and judgment *separate ourselves from within.*

EVOLVING will require *higher levels of thought and action*. The challenges of change will arrive, but also reveal our *intention to change* when we no longer choose to live in a way that doesn't support our growth.

WE create and are responsible for our own habits, the ways we choose to react, engage and be. WE also have the power to **re-create** ourselves to CHANGE, EVOLVE and BUILD *new habits* and *new ways* to respond, connect and *exist*.

TAKE ownership of the energy in your daily interactions. Energy is transferable and has the power to *unintentionally control thoughts, emotions and actions.* Choose to **remain grounded in the energy of your peace** when others choose not to be responsible for the energy they give.

Silence is a form of POWER. We can choose to crush others with our words and actions or be the ***master of ourselves*** and in control.

Forgive yourself for the behaviors you don't love within; you were **unintentionally programmed to repeat what was seen, felt and heard.**

We want our faults to be overlooked but also find it **hard to forgive the faults of others**. Choose forgiveness and love for ourselves and each other.

S peak LIFE over yourself *daily*.

THE *attributes* others love about you will also be disliked when they no longer benefit or serve their needs; **the blessing is in the clarity received to discern between real and transactional relationships.**

PROCEED in life with wisdom, don't be so quick to take action if the **vibe isn't right and aligned with your spirit**. BE PATIENT and wait until the *energy levels balance* to meet you where you are.

Never a need to **wait on others** to tell you what you want to HEAR, what you want them to SAY or DO. **Connect** to the source within to *self-serve and self-love.*

The same *energy we access* to tear each other down can also be used to **BUILD** each other up.

JOY has no requirements – *only our participation.*

We give so much attention to the emotional pains and **leave happiness out of view**. FOCUS on all there is to be grateful for and CLEAR space to let *happiness live within*.

THERE will be moments in life when you'll need to look in the mirror and *encourage yourself to bring out your best;* knowing and trusting that EVERYTHING you need **is always within.**

It's okay if not everyone sees our ***potential*** and the *vision* we see for ourselves.
BELIEVE *anyway*.

W HEN we
consistently
judge and criticize, we
blind the VISION for
others and ourselves
to GROW.

We show just as much *LOVE for ourselves* **as we do for others**, when we establish relationship boundaries that give grace, respect and compassion.

Authentically *be wonderful in*

WHO YOU ARE.

FORGIVE
what's done is done,
and what *remains is
the appreciation and
love for the lessons,
blessings and clarity*
to move life forward
with **love, grace** and
strength.

I ntentionally SET THE TONE to prepare the **life** and **vision** you see for yourself. STAY ready and present to fully experience what *shows up in life from the seeds of your trust, faith and effort.*

Remain in *love* and *grace*, as there is never a need to lower our energy level to engage with situations that don't *support* our crown and glory. **REMEMBER** *who you are* when others are trying to pull your vibration down.

ALIGNMENT
before everything.

ALWAYS treat others with **RESPECT** so you will never have the concern of *future* guilt or regrets.

GOD MAINTAINS ALL THE
RECORDS. The choice to
hold onto negative emotions
and allow them to direct our
energy, words and actions
will not erase the past.

EMOTIONS not released
take root from the seeds,
grow within our hearts and
minds, and **unconsciously
cause a repeat of the former
pain, harm or trauma.**

STRENGTH

is revealed when we are able to *remain in peace and protect our hearts, minds and spirits* during the moments when we are on the receiving end of unkind actions, words and energy.

Any act sown from the
emotion of guilt will
never reap a harvest.

When we ask to
be blessed with
the *NEXT LEVEL*
of opportunities,
relationships and an
abundance of life, we
can't expect LIFE to
**show up and unfold
in the same way.**
ALWAYS BE READY.

WE can acknowledge
the emotion from
our past pains and
disappointments;
however, we can
CHOOSE not to exist
in the emotions of a
disappointed LIFE.

ALTHOUGH the choices made by others are not what we wanted to experience, we can still choose to be respectful and kind, and *give the* GRACE **we all need** *when we too fall short.*

SELF–RELIANCE
is freedom. How
others choose to
show up for you may
never provide the
consistency, trust
and stability you
seek; **don't allow the
deficiency of others**
to make you feel less
or undermine your
value.

LOVE and
AUTHENTIC ENERGY
are the foundation for
life and all we allow to
flow from it.

It is not your
responsibility to
repair and *heal* the
LOVE, RESPECT and
TRUST that *you did
not break.*

*L*IFE WILL PROVIDE experiences that will take us out of our comfort zone and force us to ride the waves of uneasy emotions. **BE open** to receive what the *waves* are trying to teach.

FORGIVENESS
releases the barriers
in our hearts.

S TAY CONNECTED, what ***disconnects*** us will keep us from the **SOURCE** and our ability to create.

NEVER ask from others, what you REFUSE *to do for yourself.*

The **voice of our challenges** should never be louder than our *voice of solutions, faith and gratitude.*

THOSE that are
strong and
resilient, can also
be those that have
***processed and
applied the spiritual
tools*** to overcome,
peel back and release
the emotional layers
from the past.

Experiences from the past can cloud our feelings and blind us from living in the present.

KEEP HEALING.

We are meant
to laugh, love
and cry together;
*relationships are
priceless gems* that are
CONNECTED through
the life affirming
energy we give each
other and the special
bonds we create.

REMAIN OPEN to *new* life experiences that can **expand** the evolution of your growth. BLESSINGS and the *essential lessons* will show up in unexpected ways.

WORDS *have* ENERGY. SPEAK LIFE everywhere you go.

WHAT we *believe* and how we *feel* is our **VIBRATION**; it is this energy displayed in our everyday actions that ***reveals our truth***.

GOD will sometimes remove the crutches of support and celebration to *remind us that our gifts and power all come from within.* Appreciation from others is a blessing to receive; however, that does not **define** or **validate our existence**, as at any time praise can shift to judgment.

Conduct **acts of kindness without expectation.** KINDNESS is true to our spirit and not based on the emotional fluctuations of others.

ALWAYS EXPECT GOD'S *favor.*

Your ENERGY is *special*, stay **TRUE** to your own *LIGHT*.

OBSERVE THE ACTIONS, as they will always *confirm*, **reveal** and *validate* if the words spoken are TRUE.

The *intentions* behind our words are just as important as the words themselves. Be sure not confuse what you are trying to communicate by using **the wrong energy to deliver your message**.

OBSTACLES teach us what we need to learn and are a **catalyst for us to BLOOM**. *Just remember to remove the thorns from the lessons so the pain doesn't hold you hostage and stunt your growth.*

The SOLUTION will never be found if you keep *giving energy to the problem*.

BE *brave* in this life, make mistakes and learn from them. **OWN YOUR PROGRESS** and never allow the opinions of others to minimize *how to navigate your journey*. ***YOUR LIFE* belongs to you.**

*T*he MIRROR of
ourselves reflects
and projects all
we have within.
Understand that you
are not always the
cause of relationship
conflict, but the
excuse used to cover
up for someone else's
own truth of inner
turmoil, frustration
and disappointment.

OUR STORMS lead us to our destiny.

What we lose, *is as valuable* as what we have to *gain*.

*N*o regrets from the past, no worries about the future. *Live* in the ***present moment*** and make the best of today.

THERE are those SOULS that choose not to complain or project their inner emotional challenges on others. This doesn't mean problems don't exist in their life. They made the ***choice to allow*** FAITH and GRACE to guide their steps and live with a **BLESSED STATE OF MIND**.

Love of SELF
has the power to mend the hearts from any broken relationship.

EMOTIONAL WOUNDS
of the past were
reopened *not because
they were not healed,*
but because of **who
reopened** them.

EVERY CHALLENGE
we face is *designed* to
be a **spark** for us to
EVOLVE and LOVE
ourselves more.

THROUGH GRACE, the
embodiment of love,
we can *transform*
life's challenges into
growth, forgiveness
and tolerance.

Grace allows us to
lead with LOVE so we
can remain grounded
and clear.

EACH *individual soul*
evolution is different
and has its own
timing and level of
understanding. Our
growth is as **unique**
as our fingerprints,
spirit and purpose.

Being kind to those who have been unkind or toxic is not neglecting ourselves; **we neglect ourselves when we lower our vibration and change our** *ENERGY*.

YOU are the
foundation of your
own happiness, peace,
discipline, courage,
strength, passion,
freedom, health and
LOVE.

REFLECTING on the past can teach us that we have the *power to move forward*. Emotions can paralyze and make us feel like the past moment is happening in our present.

DISCERN those feelings as the **shadows** and **ghosts** of our past that we can ***forgive*** and ***release*** back to where they came from.

WE are not only our highs, ***stay humble.***

WE are not only our lows, *stay faithful.*

Have the **courage** and *confidence* to finish what your SOUL is calling you to do.

*L*OVE from a
distance is at
times necessary
to live in PEACE
with others, and give
GRACE and love to
ourselves.

We **PROJECT** not only
our fears, but also the
*dreams we have for
ourselves* when feeling
inadequate.

There is never a
need to give up on
the **VISION** we see for
ourselves, as *we are
born with everything
we need within.*

Find the OPPORTUNITY in the *midst of difficulty*.

GROWTH
is *beautiful*
because it allows
us to ***change.***

EVERY **CHOICE**
impacts our life, good
or bad; it is either a
DEPOSIT or *withdrawal.*

There will always be a ***better door to journey through*** when the door on our current path is unexpectedly closed.

A perfect life does not exist; however, we can ***choose how to use our energy, attention and focus.*** WE can choose to *create and enjoy our blessings* or remain in the realm of our challenges and temporary lows.

B^E open to adjusting your communication style so the message will not only be heard, but also *received and understood*.

LET IT GO,

or be **dragged** by it.

OUR EMOTIONS
are **sacred** –
*protect, nurture and
care for them.*

GRACE is *alchemy*.

PATIENCE *is a form of love given* in our relationships that allows each other the TIME and SPACE to *grow*.

LOVE and *RESPECT*
will ***support*** open
communication during
difficult conversations.

UNBALANCED relationships find *balance* through healthy reciprocity or natural separation because the **giver has no more to give and the taker cannot take what is no longer available**.

WE learn to move, feel and respond different when we recognize that the **LOVE WE SEEK** from others already *exists within ourselves.*

MORE time nourishing
life giving relationships;
less time engaging with
life draining relationships.

IN all exchanges,
ACCEPT **only** and *give*
honesty, respect,
authenticity and
kindness.

Our expectations of each other can never exceed our efforts.

RELATIONSHIPS require mindful effort.

BE honest with how you show up and own mishaps by sincere change.

GIVE yourself permission to be sad, angry and hurt from the disappointments of life.

All the **feelings need to be *FELT*** for us to reflect, grow, pivot and ascend.

FAITH SUPERSEDES EVERYTHING.

IF you find yourself
in a house on fire that
is soon to burn down
on and all around you,
save yourself, MAKE
PEACE and *move
beyond* from what was
and with those who
were once a part of
this journey.

An
AUTHENTIC PATH
may take longer but
the moves and impact
are ***forever legendary***.

*H*OW much we ***grow*** will be connected to the level at which we are willing to accept change.

W HAT we refuse
to accept and
acknowledge in our
mind and spirit,
our BODY will force
us to answer.

YOUR
AUTHENTIC SELF
will always be
good enough.

IDENTIFY the
feelings that are
provoked within;
these *emotions* need
your **attention**,
love and **care**.

YOU
CONTROL
the **VIBE.**

EQUALLY *give love, **forgiveness, grace, peace and compassion** to others and ourselves.*

LIFE AND DEATH

ARE IN THE POWER OF THE TONGUE;

THOSE WHO LOVE IT WILL EAT ITS FRUIT.